# Celebration Food

Clare Hibbert

Published by Evans Brothers Limited
2A Portman Mansions
Chiltern Street
London W1U 6NR

© Evans Brothers Limited 2007

Produced for Evans Brothers Limited by
White-Thomson Publishing Ltd

Printed in China by WKT Co. Ltd

Educational consultant: Sue Palmer MEd FRSA FEA
Project manager: Clare Hibbert
Picture research: Amy Sparks
Design: Balley Design Limited
Creative director: Simon Balley
Designer/Illustrator: Michelle Tilly

British Library Cataloguing in Publication Data

Hibbert, Clare 1970–
        Celebration food. - (Sparklers) 1. Festivals - Pictorial works - Juvenile
        literature 2. Food - Social aspects - Pictorial works - Juvenile literature
        3. Food habits - Pictorial works - Juvenile literature
        I. Title
        394.1

ISBN: 978 0 2375 3382 3

# Contents

# Special days

Celebrations are special days...

4

Happy birthday to you!

...when we **eat** special **food.**

5

# Spring festivals

hop

Where would you look

for Easter eggs?

6

eggs

sweets

apples

These goodies are for an Iranian spring festival.

7

# Weddings

**bride**

**groom**

This couple cut a cake at their wedding...

8

...and **this couple** share a **drink.**

9

# Harvest festival

What would **you** take to a harvest festival?

Americans **celebrate** their harvest at Thanksgiving.

# Christmas time

How would you decorate Christmas biscuits?

**Yummy!**

This **Christmas bread** looks a bit like a **crown!**

13

# Id ul-Fitr

mosque

Muslims share a feast for Id...

**dates**

**cheese-filled cakes**

...and eat sweet treats.

15

# Divali

Divali is the festival of lights.

Hindus offer food in the temple.

# Chinese New Year

People eat roast duck

at Chinese New Year...

...and give lucky tangerines as presents.

# Make it: Charoset

Mix these things together to make charoset.

- grated apples ✓
- dates and raisins ✓
- apple juice ✓
- cinnamon ✓

Mmmmm!

This **treat** is **eaten** for

Jewish Pesach.

# Notes for adults

**Sparklers** books are designed to support and extend the learning of young children. The books' high-interest subjects link in to the Early Years curriculum and beyond. Find out more about Early Years and reading with children from the National Literacy Trust (www.literacytrust.org.uk).

**Themed titles**
**Celebration Food** is one of four **Food We Eat** titles that explore food and meals from around the world. The other titles are:
**Let's eat Breakfast    Let's eat Lunch    Let's eat Dinner**

**Areas of learning**
Each **Food We Eat** title helps to support the following Foundation Stage areas of learning:
*Personal, Social and Emotional Development*
*Communication, Language and Literacy*
*Mathematical Development*
*Knowledge and Understanding of the World*
*Creative Development*

**Reading together**
When sharing this book with younger children, take time to explore the pictures together. Encourage children by asking them to find, identify, count or describe different objects. Point out different colours or textures.

Allow quiet spaces in your reading so that children can ask questions or repeat your words. Try pausing mid-sentence so children can predict the next word. This sort of participation develops early reading skills.

Follow the words with your finger as you read them aloud. The main text is in Infant Sassoon, a clear, friendly font specially designed for children learning to read and write. The labels and sound effects on the pages add fun, engage the reader and give children the opportunity to distinguish between different levels of communication. Where appropriate, labels, sound effects or main text may be presented in phonic spelling. Encourage children to imitate the sounds.

As you read the book, you can also take the opportunity to talk about the book itself with appropriate vocabulary, such as "page", "cover", "back", "front", "photograph", "label" and "page number".

You can also extend children's learning by using the books as a springboard for discussion and further activities. There are a few suggestions on the facing page.

### Pages 4–5: Special days

Give each child an outline drawing of a fairy cake to decorate and cut out. Write on the name and birthday of the child. Position on a birthday calendar mural, with the cakes sorted into the right months.

### Pages 6–7: Spring festivals

Mix crushed shredded wheat and melted chocolate and allow the children to shape the (cooled) mixture into nests to hold chicks or small chocolate eggs. Develop the theme of animal homes, for example through the song "Over in the meadow".

### Pages 8–9: Weddings

Make a model bride and groom. Use clothes pegs for bodies, wool for hair, and fabric and tissue paper for clothes and flowers.

### Pages 10–11: Harvest festival

Fill a basket with real fruits and vegetables for a harvest display. Taking turns, children can be blindfolded, take something from the basket, and then try to identify it by touch and smell.

### Pages 12–13: Christmas time

Find out what children's favourite Christmas foods are, and compile a pictorial recipe book. Decorate its cover with a collage of Christmassy angels, bells, stars and holly leaves.

### Pages 14–15: Id ul-Fitr

Id ul-Fitr marks the end of Ramadan, the Muslim month of fasting. Make hilal (crescent moon and star) decorations. Use gold foil for each star and silver foil for each moon. Use string to link them and for hanging.

### Pages 16–17: Divali

At Divali, Hindus and Sikhs light up their homes and sometimes set off fireworks. Make firework pictures. Scribble all over paper in different coloured crayons, then cover with black crayon. Use fingernails or a coin to scratch away bits of black to create a colourful firework display.

### Pages 18–19: Chinese New Year

In Chinese folk religion, each year is associated with an animal. Make cards for a pairs game, using pictures of the 12 animals: pig, rat, ox, tiger, rabbit, dragon, snake, horse, sheep, monkey, rooster and dog.

### Pages 20–21: Make it: Charoset

Pesach celebrates the escape of the Jews from slavery in Egypt. Jews eat charoset to remember the building mortar used by slaves. Use cuboid and triangular blocks to build Egyptian-style flat-roofed homes and pyramids.

# IndeX

**Picture acknowledgements:**
**Alamy:** 7 (Richard Levine), 9 (Photo Network), 10 (archivberlin/Fotoagentur/GmbH), 17 (ArkReligion.com); **Corbis:** 4–5 (Fabio Cardoso), 6 (© Ariel Skelley/Blend Images), 11 (Larry Williams), 12 (Ralf Hirschberger/dpa), 14 (Kazuyoshi Nomachi), 16 (Ken Seet), 19 (Franklin Lau); **Getty:** 8 (Ryan McVay/Stone); **iStockphoto:** cover balloons (Vasiliki Varvaki), cover tablecloth, 2–3, 13, 22–24 (Jon Helgason), cover, 13 (Andres Balcazar), cover sky, 22–24 (Judy Foldetta), 15 (Paul Cowan), 15 tablecloth (Gaffera); **Photolibrary:** 18 (Peter Brooks), 20–21 (Foodpix).